Aşk Mafia: Armor of The World

Abhijit Naskar is the 21st century Neuroscientist and Poet who has been serving at the forefront of humankind's struggle against inhumanity. As an untiring advocate of mental health and global harmony, he became a beloved best-selling author across the world with his very first book "The Art of Neuroscience in Everything". With his revolutionary contributions in Cognitive and Behavioral Neuroscience Naskar has helped the world tackle the horrors of biases, stereotypes, discrimination, hate, intolerance and fanaticism more effectively, because of which he is lovingly hailed by humankind as 'the humanitarian scientist'.

Aşk Mafia

Armor of The World

ABHIJIT
NASKAR

Lives to Serve Before I Sleep
When Humans Unite: Making A World Without Borders
All For Acceptance
Monk Meets World
Mission Reality
Citizens of Peace: Beyond The Savagery of Sovereignty
Operation Justice: To Make A Society That Needs No Law
See No Gender
The Gospel of Technology
Every Generation Needs Caretakers: The Gospel of
Patriotism
Aşkanjali: The Sufi Sermon
Mad About Humans: World Maker's Almanac
Revolution Indomable
When Call The People: My World My Responsibility
No Foreigner Only Family
Hurricane Humans: Give me accountability, I'll give you
peace
Ain't Enough to Look Human
Servitude is Sanctitude
Time To End Democracy: The Meritocratic Manifesto
I Vicdansaadet Speaking: No Rest Till The World is Lifted
Boldly Comes Justice: Sentient not Silent
Good Scientist: When Science and Service Combine
Sleepless for Society
Neden Türk: The Gospel of Secularism
Martyr Meets World: To Solve The Hard Problem of
Inhumanity
The Shape of A Human: Our America Their America
When Veins Ignite: Either Integration or Degradation
Heart Force One: Need No Gun to Defend Society
Solo Standing on Guard: Life Before Law
Generation Corazon: Nationalism is Terrorism
Mucize Insan: When The World is Family
Hometown Human: To Live For Soil and Society
Girl Over God: The Novel
Gente Mente Adelante: Prejudice Conquered is World
Conquered
Earthquakin' Egalitarian: I Die Everyday So Your Children
Can Live
Giants in Jeans: 100 Sonnets of United Earth
Vatican Virus: The Forbidden Fiction (Abi Naskar
Adventures Book 2)
Karadeniz Chronicle: The Novel (Abi Naskar Adventures

Book 3)
Şehit Sevda Society: Even in Death I Shall Live
Handcrafted Humanity: 100 Sonnets For A Blunderful
World
Mücadele Muhabbet: Gospel of An Unarmed Soldier
Making Britain Civilized: How to Gain Readmission to The
Human Race
Dervish Advaitam: Gospel of Sacred Feminines and Holy
Fathers
Honor He Wrote: 100 Sonnets For Humans Not Vegetables
The Gentalist: There's No Social Work, Only Family Work
Either Reformist or Terrorist: If You Are Terror I Am Your
Grandfather
Woman Over World: The Novel (Abi Naskar Adventures
Book 4)
High Voltage Habib: Gospel of Undoctrination
Bulldozer on Duty
Find A Cause Outside Yourself: Sermon of Sustainability
Ingan Impossible: Handbook of Hatebusting
Amor Apocalypse: Canım Sana İhtiyacım
Amantes Assemble: 100 Sonnets of Servant Sultans
Mucize Misafir Merhaba: The Peace Testament
Divane Dynamite: Only truth in the cosmos is love
Sin Dios Sí Hay Divinidad: The Pastor Who Never Was
Corazon Calamidad: Obedient to None, Oppressive to None
Esperanza Impossible: 100 Sonnets of Ethics, Engineering &
Existence
Mukemmel Musalman: Kafir Biraz, Peygamber Biraz
Himalayan Sonneteer: 100 Sonnets of Unsubmission
Yarasistan: My Wounds, My Crown
The Centurion Sermon: Mental Por El Mundo
Her Insan Ailem: Everyone is Family, Everywhere is Home
Humankind, My Valentine: World's First Anthology of 1000
Sonnets

DEDICATION

Bu kitap artık sana adanmıştır.
Kendine iyi bak, Berra!

CONTENTS

Part 1: Preface

What is secularism? Secularism is but the rightful manifestation of religion - civilized manifestation of religion.

Because secularism acknowledges, and more importantly, embraces all religions without boasting about the supremacy one over the others.

To put it simply - secularism is but religion in practice. Secularism is the rightful absolution of religion - not this religion and that religion, but every religion - the source religion - that is, love.

Secularism is christianity in practice - when you truly and genuinely love your neighbor.

Secularism is islam in practice - when you truly and genuinely hope for the peace of all.

Secularism is judaism in practice - when you feel responsible for the welfare of others.

Secularism is hinduism or sanatana dharma in practice - when you forget all divide between mind and mind.

Secularism is buddhism in practice - when everyone lives in harmony, without resisting each other's unique identity.

Then how come such a simple act of harmony and true religiousness is almost always deemed as blasphemy by the so-called advocates of organized religion, that is, the fundamentalists!

All through history, as well as in present times, religion is greatly endorsed and practiced as an affair with doctrines, while in reality, true, spiritful, mindful and heartful religion is anything but that.

True religion is a love affair with the spirit within, not with the picket fences that we place around the spirit – true religion is a love affair with the spirit of universality within the human heart everywhere, not with an imaginary spirit in an imaginary heaven.

As I once said - interfaith is faith supreme. In fact, there is no such thing as interfaith communication, there is just human communication. Because interfaith alone is human, all other fundamentalist behavior of faith is anything but human - as such, it is anything but faith.

To take it further - in a society of true religion, faith and interfaith should be one and the same - when they are not, it only means that we study religion wrong - that is, we are yet to understand religion.

Religion and religious harmony should be one and the same - yet they are not. Why? Because we don't have religion, what we have is counterfeit religion - counterfeits in different forms - forms that refuse to even acknowledge the possibility, that they are all but mere microscopic reflections of something that can't even be put in forms - that can't be organized.

Religion organized is religion lost, fervor indoctrinated is fervor ruined. Or to put it simply - integration is religion, all else is a very, very distant echo.

Which means that - when you ask, what is religion, if you are thinking in terms of this religion and that religion, then you are not actually concerned with religion in the first place, you are only inquiring about its primeval counterparts.

In civilized religion there is no division - whatever bears division is anything but religion - whatever bears division is anything but civilized.

Our objective is to surpass the very concept of secularism - our objective is to step into the nameless valley, where the very construct of division is but a distant memory. Many so-called advocates of religion may call it blasphemy or crime against god - I call it the civilized evolution of the human mind - I call it the rightful progression of religion – I call it the realization of god.

But the point is, it is not an objective that we can reach at some point in the future. Rather it ought to be the very starting point of all our endeavors at this very moment.

Not aim for nondivision, we gotta start from nondivision - not aim for secularism, we gotta start from secularism - not aim for harmony, we gotta start from harmony.

Harmony is the starting point - integration is the starting point - universal acceptance is the starting point. It is this simple, yet why do we complicate it with so much intellectual jargon, like existentialism, empiricism, humanism and so on!

Why can't the human simply be human!

A real existentialist pays attention to existence, not to existentialism. A real empiricist pays attention to the rightful use of empirical evidence, not to mere empiricism. A real humanist pays attention to a life of human substance, not to shallow theoretical concepts like humanism.

Faith is a simple thing - why do we complicate it so! When it is dark, hold on to the light within. That's faith! When things get tough, muster the force of perseverance within. That's faith!

It's never about division, yet that's what we've made faith all about. What a pity!

Part 2

Friday Azaan and Sunday Choir,
All pray to the same light.
Yet in our divisive stupidity,
We use it as excuse to maintain divide.

Division inside causes division outside,
Over time that division becomes the norm.
Take off the blinkers of illusive faith,
So you may witness the lightful dawn.

Sapiens is the dawn,
Sapiens is the saint.
Sapiens is the bridge of heart,
Sapiens is the mend.

Ain't there nothing sapiens can't do,
Ain't no mountain sapiens can't climb.
Ain't no darkness sapiens can't conquer,
Ain't no division sapiens can't undivide.

Sapiens is the antithesis of division,
Human is the antithesis of hate.
If human and integration are not the same,
It is a society of the unsapient dead.

Human and inclusion are one and the same,
Human and harmony are one and the same.
Human means a willful defiance of hate,
Human means celebrating each other's lane.

You can be a believer and still be human,
You can be an atheist and still be human.
You can be whatever and still be human,
But there's no such thing as a fundamentalist human.

Secularism has three stages.
First, you realize, all religions
pray to the same God.
Second, you realize, God exists
only in the human heart.

Finally, all talk of God disappears,
and what remains among the humans,
is a natural sense of oneness.

Instead of pouring milk
on a lifeless stone,
pour it in a hungry stomach.
Instead of lighting candle
at a lifeless altar,
light it in a helpless heart.

Above the human, all is illusion,
Below the human, all is delusion.
One who knows the use of both,
Is the rightful voice of reason.

Every heart holds a voice,
But tradition keeps it shunned.
Every skull holds a brain,
But society keeps it barred.

Every spine holds a backbone,
But peer pressure turns it into jello.
Every body holds a conscientious being,
But society conditions it to be callow.

Be the being of balance and bravery,
Be the being of conscience and capacity.
Be the being no one expects you to be,
Be the impossible height of humanity.

Be the paradigm-breaking anomaly,
That elevates all of humankind.
Be the epoch-shattering anchor,
That tethers time to light.

15 **Part 3**

16

Water has to be the right temperature,
For it to appease our human thirst.
Too cold, it'll give you frost-bite,
Too hot, and it'll burn your throat.

Intellect has to be rightly moderated,
For it to push mind and society upward.
Too little, it facilitates superstition,
Too much, and it turns the mind cold.

I'd rather be a know-nothing idiot,
Than an intellectual retard.
I'd rather die with character intact,
Than live with character in the mud.

You may wonder, what's the connection,
between intellect and character!
The connection is that, unmoderated intellect
often is an impediment to character.

Science without warmth
is intellectual con,
Faith without warmth
causes nothing but mourn.

What's The Difference
(Sonnet 1037)

If a scientist has no humility,
what's the difference between
a scientist and a computer!
If a doctor has no warmth,
what's the difference between
a doctor and a butcher!

If a teacher has no curiosity,
what's the difference between
a teacher and a circus trainer!
If a filmmaker has no originality,
what's the difference between
a filmmaker and a photocopier!

If a cop cannot practice self-correction,
what's the difference between
a cop and an executioner!
If a theologian has no integrative spirit,
what's the difference between
a theologian and a mumbling parrot!

If a modern human cannot balance reason and warmth,
what's the difference between a sentient human
and a creature from the swamp!

I get visions of words,
But it ain't nothing supernatural.
It's just a natural expression,
of divergently wired circuits neural.

Much of my literary universe
is born of intense transcendental states.
Had I let it overwhelm my common sense,
I'd've risen a supernatural figurehead.

Instead, I looked for a tangible explanation,
that flatters my curiosity, not ignorance.
Thus, I stumbled upon the neurochemical roots,
from which all normal and paranormal manifest.

Mind is not a gateway to another realm,
Mind is a wondrous universe on its own.
The messages we think we get from the heavens,
Are actually subconscious constructs of our own.

Be conscious of consciousness,
but more of your subconsciousness.
Your eyes will open up to new vistas,
with wider and more meaningful sapience.

Part 4

You can't pursue consciousness,
You are consciousness.
You can't pursue awareness,
You are awareness.

Awareness is not a means to an end,
Awareness is the means as well as the end.
Awareness is the alpha, awareness is omega,
Where there is no awareness, there is no existence.

Awareness comes through purpose,
Purpose comes through awareness.
Life lived with purpose,
Is life lived with awareness.

Awareness is everything,
Without awareness there is nothing.
I ain't talkin' 'bout reality independent of mind,
But about reality born of our neural functioning.

Our reality is our responsibility.
No extraterrestrial force
is gonna humanize it for us.
Our life is our decision,
Nobody can draw the lines for us.

Control your habits, control your stress.
Restrain your biases, restrain disparities.
Correction is the first step of excellence.
Correct yourself, you'll course correct humanity.

Reason is the bridge between you and the future,
Love is the bridge between you and real sanity.
Love is the bridge between you and the world,
You are the bridge between humans and humanity.

Live to love, love to live,
All else is trivial.
Till you find the world inside,
You are but an animal.

All are born human,
Very few die human.
All receive a human life,
Very few live the life of human.

I don't want you to follow me,
I want you to be a better version of me.
Be original, be an inspiration,
Be a beacon upon the fabric of society.

The older I get,
the younger I get.
Either you live or don't,
there is no death.

Death implies that you lived once,
But if you truly live,
you'll keep living in people's heart.
Once alive, always alive!
Only the unborn fret about doing part.

When you live, you have no time for death,
Life keeps you busy enough to worry about fiction.
Little insecurity will always be there, that's okay,
Just don't let it cripple your resolve and conviction.

Live, live and live again,
Live beyond the life of your ancestors.
Live life and be a beacon of life,
You become beacon when you live with purpose.

When you live with purpose,
Every nerve in your body comes alive.
Purpose is the compass,
Without which all nerves and veins go awry.

27

Part 5

Love of purpose and purpose of love,
That's what defines a human being.
Being of love and love of being,
That's the civilized way of existing.

Once a lover, always a lover,
whether that love is reciprocated.
Once you love someone,
they become your responsibility for life,
whether you are together or separated.

Don't seek for someone you can talk sense with,
Seek for someone you can talk nonsense with.
One who turns you into a clumsy fool,
They are indeed the one to spend your life with.

If everyone fell in love,
there won't be any church in the world.
Once you fall in love,
all faith, state and class will disappear.

I am in love with the world,
and it is love that conquers all.
Try to conquer hearts not lands,
and yours will be the whole world.

The world is a sucker for a human,
But most live life as a walking label.
Take off all labels and throw 'em in the bin,
Light up the world as a beacon indivisible.

Write from joy, you'll make five friends.
Write from pain, the world will make you family.
Write from head, you'll make a name.
Write from heart, you'll remake reality.

Mutluluktan yaz, beş kişi arkadaşın olsun.
Yaralardan yaz, tüm dünya ailen olsun.
Beyinden yaz, biraz şan ve şöhret bulacaksın,
Kalbinden yaz, tüm kâinat sana aşık olsun.

Culture begins with kindness.
No kindness, no culture.
Religion begins with kindness.
No kindness, no religion.

Culture is but a vessel -
appearance varies across geography,
but the force within is one and the same.

Naskar is the outcome of such churning.
When all cultures come together, Naskar is born.
Call it Naskar, call it Human - all the same,
It all represents the undivided spirit of dawn.

When you bring down the barriers,
you not only become a universal human,
your capacities expand a thousand folds.
To a divided mind what I do is magic,
but I am not the first one,
history is full with such souls.

My mind can come up with pearls,
because I don't clutter it with
junk like luxury and creed.
I live simple, I think creedless,
thus everything I do seems magic.

Wipe out India, and you wipe out the land,
that gave birth to me.
Wipe out America, and you wipe out the land,
that made me a household name.
Wipe out Turkey, and you wipe out the land,
that kept me soaked in love.
Wipe out Latin America, and you wipe out the land,
that showed me the passion lane.

Part 6

34

Passion is the supreme science,
Without passion even science is impotent.
But pure passion without some reason
inadvertently leads to hate and intolerance.

Always keep balance in life,
between passion and reason.
Reason without warmth is knife without handle,
the same holds true for warmth without reason.

Reason where reason is needed,
throw logic to wind if it is the human thing to do.
Defy logic when logic is inhuman,
but when superstition wreaks havoc,
wield all your rationality anew.

Wield all your faculties for collective good,
Do what's right for your age and time.
Let neither past nor future dictate righteousness,
Righteousness of the moment comes from veins alive.

Her an, herkese,
Her gün, her gece,
Ailen gibi bakmalı.
İnsan olarak doğdun,
İnsan gibi yaşamalı.

Day and night, night and day,
This moment now,
And every moment far away,
Love each and love all,
Save love there's no other way.
Ain't enough to be born a human,
To find life we gotta give our life away.

Cada día, cada noche,
En todos momentos de la vida,
Tenemos tratar a todos como familia.
Nacimos humanos, viviremos humanos,
El buen mundo nace de la intención buena.

Unless you are protective of the world
like you are protective of your family,
nothing will ever change.
Unless you feel responsible for the welfare
of every single person you come across,
the world will never have a moment of wellness.

Kusursuz bir dünya kusurzuz bir kalpten doğar,
Flawless world is born of flawless heart.
There's no such thing as a flawless society,
But what's to stop us from making it
a less inhuman world!

Right world is born of right intention,
Right intention is born of accountability.
Humanity is the proof of accountability,
Accountability is the proof of humanity.

Humanity is the proof of life,
Life is the proof of humanity.
Where there is heart, there is life,
Where there is life, there is humanity.

Light is the proof of heart,
Heart is the proof of light.
Breath is a vessel for acceptance,
Acceptance is an act of love and life.

Love is but a record of time,
Time is but a record of love.
Love is the bane, love is the boon,
Love is what takes us lightward.

Konuşmak istedin - konuştum.
Susmamı istedin - sustum.
İnsanların mutluluğu için,
Benim de duygular var - unuttum.

I use English when understanding is needed,
I use Turkish when I wanna remain unheard.
Some languages are vessels for the head,
Some tongues are born to bear the heart.

Part 7

Birine güvenmek ayıp değil,
Güvensiz hayat, nasıl hayat!
Bin kere ihanete uğra, ayıp değil,
Be the cure, not cause, of mistrust.

Let all mistrust be aimed at you,
Don't let them turn you bitter.
Resist not the cruel waves of the sea,
Befriending the waves you'll rise as sailor.

Tears are portal to strength,
Insecurity is portal to invincibility.
Brood not when you are depressed,
Activity alleviates anxiety.

Solitude facilitates creativity,
Obscurity facilitates genius.
My most productive years are my loneliest years,
My vagabond years prepared the soul
to conquer the world.

When your heart breaks, let it break,
Don't try to resist the shattering pieces.
It is from the abyss of burning misery,
Greatness emerges as phoenix from the ashes.

Love is The Bane
(The Sonnet)

Love is the boon,
Love is the bane.
Love is relief,
Love is the pain.

From love will come your troubles,
From love will rise your answer.
You'll fail in love, you'll fly in love,
In love's insanity your sight will clear.

Love is torture,
Love is disaster.
Love exposes the counterfeits,
While it purifies the lover.

In a world run by calculating coldness,
be the anomaly of love insensible.
Cure for this anemic world,
is your love impossible.

Land of love bears no belief and disbelief,
Land of love knows no, 'my culture, your culture'.
Land of love is the antithesis of stereotypes,
Land of love is run on acceptance and dialogue.

Dialogue means more listening, less talking.
Dialogue means more learning, less judging.
Dialogue is the antithesis of assumption.
Dialogue means no demonizing, no dehumanizing.

Let me put this into perspective.

Yes, I am a muslim poet, I am also humankind's pinnacle of peace and reason. I have done more for integration and humanitarianism than most writers, scholars, and philosophers in history. Now tell me - what were you saying about, all muslims being terrorists!

Yes, I am a latin lover, I am also an epitome of human rights. I have done more for science-based justice and righteousness than most social scientists and political philosophers in history. Now tell me - what were you saying about, all Latinos being drug mules!

These are just two of the many examples. Still if you don't get the point of it all, then throw the book in the trash already, because the next bit of poetry will make even less sense to the bigoted.

45

Part 8

Chrismadan
(The Sonnet)

What happens when two ancient cultures come together!
They create a spectacular specimen called dervish advaitin.
When mistletoe and menorrah combine, heart shines brighter,
Beyond belief 'n disbelief, there's a land most enlightening.

Keep your outdated sectarian identities to yourself,
I am Jewistian, Hinduslim, or simply Human Universal.
Be the next civilized step of humankind's evolution,
Not just another savage vessel of mistakes ancestral.

Revitalized by Ramadan, humanized by Christmas,
Let's celebrate Chrismadan, as well as Hanukkawali.
Instead of carrying on as second-hand savages,
Habibi come, let us start living with humanity!

When all religions combine, a modern human is born.
Without integration there is no dawn, just endless mourn.

For the world to have integration,
We gotta choose integration over tribalism.
For the world to have love and harmony,
We gotta choose love over hate and nationalism.

But the point is, you don't choose love,
Love chooses you, and changes you for good.
Open your heart and submit to love,
Thus you sow the seeds of good.

The highest truth of life can only be realized,
If your heart lives in the land of love.
I am not talkin' about having a partner by your side,
To live in love means to see love and be love.

But mark you, love is not about eternal laughter,
Nor is it about a mythical life without disaster.
Love is but a pleasurable pandemonium,
To love is to live with people
through sweet and messy everafter.

Loneliness Psychology
(No-Nonsense Sonnet)

Being happy alone is no sign of genius,
It is either narcissism or hypocrisy.
You've got to be extremely selfish,
To be happy without human company.

If your heart is alive and human,
Loneliness will cause you misery.
It's only the self-absorbed animal,
Who don't need people to be happy.

It's okay if you are alone and miserable,
It is but a healthy mind's healthy reaction.
Do not romanticize it with phony philosophy,
For derangement starts with self-deception.

Fact of the matter is - I suffer, therefore I am.
Life is but a cosmic dance between dusk and dawn.

Study the dusk, you'll wake up to dawn.
Study the dark, you'll understand light.
Study the pain, you'll understand joy.
Study your weakness, you'll know your might.

Study your wounds, you'll discover medicine.
Study your failures, you'll know your forte.
Study your dread, you'll find determination.
Study atrocities, you'll find the human way.

Let me put this into perspective
with a hard-to-bear truth.
If you can't bear the harshness of truth,
you can never humanize the global hood.

Behind every man alive and kicking,
there is a woman.
Behind every woman abused and killed,
there is a man.

Unless you realize that society has
a toxic masculinity problem,
there'll be no justice, no equality.
Unless the humans realize their bestiality,
there'll never be any actual humanity.

Part 9

Acknowledging inhumanity
is the beginning of humanity.
To acknowledge you are animal,
is birth of the human.

None of us are actually human,
We are all human in the making.
Till we realize this simple fact,
There is no actual peacemaking.

Peace begins with non-judgment,
Peace is another name for integration.
Integrated we rise, segregated we disintegrate,
No advancement is advancement without assimilation.

I am a Christian to the Christian,
a Jew to the Jew, a Muslim to the Muslim,
a Hindu to the Hindu, an atheist to the atheist,
but the brightest nightmare to the intolerant fiend.

The opposite of intolerance is not toleration,
The opposite of intolerance is assimilation.
We've long crossed the time when
mere tolerance was a matter of glory,
now it is time for unification.

O beni kral sanıyor,
ama gerçek bu değil,
çünkü fakir gibi yaşıyorum.
Herkese ben güç verdim ama,
güçlü bir el tutmak için,
uzun zamandır ölüyorum.

If you feel the will to go out of your way,
to fathom what I say in a different tongue,
that right there is the first sign,
that you've developed the spirit of integration -
the spirit of unification.

No act is more civilized
than the act of unification.
Where there is unification
there is civilization.

Between humans, nonsense like color,
creed, orientation do not matter.
It's only the animals that prioritize
divisive tradition over character.

So I say, be human,
even if you're branded traitor.
Better branded traitor by animals,
than compromise your human character.

57

Part 10

Yazar olmak çok kolay
Yazar kalmak kolay değil.
Aşık olmak çok kolay,
Aşık kalmak kolay değil.

Acıyor, yine de yazıyor!
Yazarın en büyük gücü yaralarıdır.
Surf your wounds, don't serve them,
Only the wounded emerges as wound-rider.

Heart breaking is heart in making,
Wounds bleeding are wonders in making.
Weakness is but strength in making.
Darkness is but light in making.

Life is but death in making,
Death is but life in making.
Rise above all life and death,
Learn to live beyond the living.

Beyond the dead and the undead,
there is a valley of life.
You shall find me there,
where neither happiness nor misery,
but love is the measure of life.

Are you in love?
Yes.
Are you in pain?
Always.
Are you happy?
Always.
In awe they ask me,
how can you be all at once!
I smile, and respond,
because I am alive.

The Pillar
(A Sonnet)

People come, spend some time with me,
Then they leave and go their own way.
Some leave bidding a sweet goodbye,
Then there're times I get trashed away.

To the world I am but a pillar,
I've accepted that role in society.
But secretly the heart wreaks havoc,
Not being able to hold on to somebody.

There is no cure for my condition,
It's the price a reformer has to pay.
No world is lifted without sacrifice,
That's how the being becomes a gateway.

Be a shelter to others in their times of agony.
Once you've fulfilled your role in their life,
Do not be a hindrance to their joy and liberty.

Part 11

Lovers don't belong to themselves,
To be alive means to love and to enable.
Reformers don't belong to themselves,
Life of a reformer belongs to the people.

Reformers don't belong to nations,
Reformers belong to the world.
Reformers don't belong to one culture,
Reformers belong to time eternal.

Once you choose to take up that duty,
Once you choose to be the armor of the people,
That's the end of an individualistic life,
And the beginning of a collectivist vessel.

Being a reformer doesn't mean
mere marching on the streets,
Being a reformer doesn't mean
yelling at every little incompetency.
Being a reformer means living a responsible life,
Being a reformer means engaging in
everyday little acts of humanity.

Let me put this into perspective with a few examples.

Buy less and buy local, and you'll facilitate
a sustainable and healthy economy.
Save trees, buy ebooks, for thus
you facilitate a diseasefree society.

Save Trees, Buy Ebooks
(The Sonnet)

Oh, I know so well, the euphoria of bibliosmia!
So, buy only the priceless books in printed form.
If explorers of knowledge don't act responsible,
All glory of bibliophilia is fraudulent and wrong.

Literature is just the same, no matter the format,
You gotta prioritize between ebooks and print form.
In pursuit of knowledge ebooks are environment-friendly,
Therefore, keep your print book buying to bare minimum.

We cherish music totally electronically these days,
We no longer clutter the shelves with CDs or vinyls.
Why not do the same with literature, especially when,
Ebooks are to print books what EVs are to gas vehicles.

Printed books will always be special, so buy one book
by your favorite author in print, rest in digital form.
Save trees, buy ebooks, that's the new book lovers' norm.

Be responsible, and live responsible,
that's the only kind of human there is.
Be a lover, and stay a lover,
that's the only civilized life there is.

But remember one thing.

Human course is a thorny course,
An act of humanity attracts more mockery
than a lifetime of inhumanity.
Stand strong without compromise,
upon your conviction flourishes society.

When it gets too rough,
take stock of the strength within.

How?

Here's how.

No matter what you do or say,
You cannot obstruct sunrise.
Each ridicule only rejuvenates me,
They trigger me to shine bright.

The more you mock, the higher I fly,
More you ignore, more evident I become.
Every act of hate ends up feeding my light,
More you persecute, more immortal I become.

Part 12

Kill me, I'll still be immortal.
Kiss me, I'll die on the spot.
Hate me, I'll still be a legend.
Hug me, I'll wipe out myself
without a word.

Love me, hate me, it's all in my favor.
If you love me, I'm in your heart.
If you hate me, I'm in your fervor.

Thus speaks the reformer responsible,
On whose shoulders the world awakens.
Let all bad blood end with you,
Look at the haters through the eyes of a guardian.

Reformer is the guardian,
Reformer is the parent.
Reformer is the ruler,
Reformer is the servant.

Reformer holds no allegiance to ideology,
Reformer holds no allegiance to culture.
Reformer doesn't have such primitive luxury,
Reformer's sight draws the humanitarian picture.

For example, reformer sees and feels thus.

Wipe out America, you wipe out innovation.
Wipe out India, you wipe out spirituality.
Wipe out Latin America, you wipe out liberty.
Wipe out Turkiye, you wipe out poetry.

I want it all, every nation, every culture.
Insects may be satisfied with one culture,
I am a human being, I need the whole world.

Such sight of assimilation is impossible,
unless you renounce your tribal allegiance.
Either you stay tribal your whole life,
or you finally stand up as a real sapiens.

See the whole, without reservation,
See the good in all as well as bad.
Then work to empower the good,
while rejecting every last trace of the bad.

Human being is the antidote,
Human being is transformer.
Defying death as dynamite,
We shall dawn as global armor.

Take the world on your shoulders,
Let their tears run through your blood.
Let their agony saturate your lungs,
Only then shall you emerge as vanguard.

When the world lives in your every pore,
When you find joy in easing their woe,
When their struggle becomes your struggle,
The world will open for you every door.

When human heart becomes a human shelter,
Not a single soul will ever go homeless.
When life of a human is lived for the humans,
Not a single life will ever feel helpless.

Be the human none could never be,
Be the soul no sapiens knows nothing of.
Be the gateway to a hateless world,
Be humankind's way out of this heartless muck.

Tap your heart, for heart is the tap,
Torrents of which will wash all hate away.
Map your brain, for brain is the map,
That'll direct us in the biasless way.

Part 13

Turn your heart into a gospel,
and you won't need any other gospel.
Turn your conscience into constitution,
and you won't be slave to no legal rumble.

Outsourcing rightness is an act of wrongness,
Outsourcing morality is the ruin of morality.
If you must live, live original, otherwise,
There's no point in second-hand existentiality.

Breaths we breathe are ancestral handouts,
Thoughts we think are ancestral leftovers.
Scraping leftovers the mind falls sick,
Then the sick mind causes further social disasters.

We sustain disaster in the guise of norm,
Sensibility seems like deviation from tradition.
We make senselessness the regular way of life,
Act of reason feels like existential devastation.

So we continue, as an ignorant and intolerant species,
With more counterfeit knowledge than real knowledge.
Worst of all is that we pass prejudice as wisdom,
While we deem act of assimilation as sacrilege.

It's a great tragedy,
when love becomes sacrilege,
and hate is deemed sacred.
Love thy neighbor comes
with ethnic criteria,
while welfare comes with a price tag.

A complete overhaul is long overdue,
of everything we conceive as civilized.
It's time to scrutinize all we believe,
Often our belief is what keeps us uncivilized.

There is no perception without bias, yet,
Biaslessness oughta be the aim of perception.
We can never be fully free from biases,
But in trying so we shall become less inhuman.

The point is not to create a biasless utopia,
But at least we can bring the biases in control.
When biases are controlled, divisions are contained,
When divisions are contained, all will be whole.

Languages come easy to me,
Cultures come easy to me,
Scriptures come easy to me,
Science comes easy to me.
You know why?
Because there is no me,
only the mission of undivided humanity.

I don't drink,
I don't smoke,
I don't do drugs,
I don't watch sports.

I am too high on my mission,
to be enslaved by cheap thrills.
To ensure, there is a dawn tomorrow,
the Reformer stands sleepless,
with a backbone well hinged.

Backbone is the being,
Mind is the mission.
Conscience is character,
Rigidity is prison.

Nerves make us individual,
Sweat makes us sapient.
Brain gives us power,
Heart makes us sentient.

Part 14

Omniscience is fiction,
But you need not know all.
Know the truth of love,
All that matters will be well.

That's all you need to know,
Rest will come on its own.
Know love and live love,
The world will usher into dawn.

Where there is determination, there is dawn,
Where the human gives up, dusk looms.
Where there is dignity, there is character,
Where there is character, heart blooms.

There is no heart,
if there is no character.
There is no character,
if there is no heart.

We need brains to build the world,
But first we gotta envision with heart.
Brain's vision runs cold over time,
Heart's vision provides eternal warmth.

Where there is warmth, there is poetry,
Where there is poetry, there is life.
Where there is life, there is integration,
Where there is integration, there is light.

Light is but another name for integration,
Darkness is but synonym for divide.
Defy division, you defy darkness,
Practice integration, you cause light.

Light is possible because you are possible,
Peace is possible because you are possible.
But peace is poetry only a human can fathom,
To sectarian savages all this is incomprehensible.

Nature is poetry only a naturalist can fathom,
Science is poetry only a scientist can fathom.
Math is poetry only a mathematician can fathom,
Love is poetry only a lover can fathom.

To fathom love you gotta be love,
To fathom peace you gotta be peace.
Civilization begins with realization,
Realization springs from heart without leash.

No heart, no realization,
No realization, no civilization.
No poetry, no civilization,
No civilization, no realization.

No pain, no poetry -
Take no pain, make no civilization.
Failure is the fulcrum of success,
Sacrifice is the fulcrum of civilization.

Dünyayı inşa etmek
gerçek bir insan için kolaydır.
Çünkü bir amaç için ölmek
amaçsız yaşamaktan daha saygındır.

Morir por un propósito
es más honorable
que vivir sin propósito.
Morir como humano
es más honorable
que dormir como insecto.

Indifference may define insect life,
But indifference is disgrace
to human life and human society.
If you wanna find a human
when you look into the mirror,
you gotta stop adjusting to inhumanity.

Part 15

88

Adjusting to inhumanity is to practice inhumanity.
Complying with corruption is to advocate corruption.
Stand your ground of humanity despite all hate -
I'm mocked and hated up to my neck,
yet do you find me compromising my conviction!

Despite all their hate and envy,
I'll still be the world's first multicultural poet.
Despite their divisive insurrections,
I'll still be a beacon of oneness.

All mockery aimed at your sense of humanity,
ends up but enhancing your sense of humanity.
Guardians of society shouldn't be bothered
by the tantrums of children -
Stand firm, stand fervent, ignoring indignity!

Reputation is for civilians -
We are reformers, we don't have such luxury.
Reformers are civilians too,
but an epoch making demonstration
of evolving citizenry.

Valor runs bountiful in our blood,
Society persecutes that valor, and peddles icewater.
As doting parent you gotta guide the society
in a humane direction,
dragging it gently by the ear.

Kanımda akıyor tüm kâinat,
Her güç gönlümden doğar.
Benim nasip benim ellerimde,
Her medeniyet niyetten doğar.

Each corpuscle contains the cosmos,
each valve is gateway to valor.
What this world needs
is not character-crushing prejudice,
but prejudice-defying character.

What this world needs is,
not termite producing tradition,
but might producing tradition.
What our society needs is,
not fright producing paradigm,
but flight producing paradigm.

Updating your phone means nothing,
if fervor is stuck in stoneage.
Buying a Tesla means nothing,
if the mind on driver's seat
is an Edison like savage.

Mobile phone can mobilize the mind,
it can also immobilize the mind -
All depends on how you use it.
Greatest of tool gets corrupt,
in the hands of a primitive.

Ain't enough to live as a person,
We gotta live as a possibility.
Or rather, amidst all pathetic possibilities,
It's time to burn bright,
as a poetically glaring impossibility.

Be the poetry the world can't fathom,
Be the reason the world can't handle.
Their opinion of you is not your problem,
You gotta uphold, not applause, but principle.

Uphold principle, not prejudice.
Uphold reason, not rigidity.
Uphold duty, not derangement.
Uphold correction, not conformity.

Conform to no inkling ancestral,
Conform to no habit historical.
Conform to no force external,
Submit only to love universal.

Part 16

Submit to no definition of love,
Submit to the act of love.
Be swayed by no perfectionist fiction,
Lose all in the messy reality of love.

Embracing the pain of love,
You become worthy of the joy of love.
Bearing the devastation of heartbreak,
You become the rightful bearer of heart.

Heart is not something you are born with,
You gotta earn it through your action.
Walking the agonizing course of selflessness,
We dawn as the rightful human under the sun.

Dolor es mi poder,
Heridas mi corona.
Amando a los que nos odian,
Levantamos con humanidad verdadera.

Heridas del humano son corona del corazón.
More you bludgeon me,
more I burn with a cosmic glow.

Despite the noises,
Despite the compulsions,
Despite the lack of silver spoon,
Despite all third world obstructions -
If a dropout vagabond could do so much,
What holds you back from expansion!

But, please, I beg of you,
Don't turn me into yet another
spiritual guru imported from the East.
Don't be a second-hand Naskar -
Expand to such an extent,
that even Naskar turns obsolete.

The day Naskar becomes obsolete,
I'll know I've fulfilled my mission.
Surpassing Naskar consciousness,
is the fulfillment of Naskarean vision.

Surpassing Naskar consciousness
is fulfillment of Naskar consciousness.
Surpassing Naskar consciousness
is the beginning of Naskar consciousness.

Come down to the soil,
the soil will teach you how to serve the soil.
Come down to human streets,
the streets will teach you
how to fight for human rights.

World, my valentine,
or to be specific -
Humankind, my valentine,
Come hell or high water!
Hurt me, I'll walk away,
Hurt people, and I'll be your
worst nightmare.

I am the nightmare,
I am the daybreak.
Differences I accept heartily,
Discrimination makes my calm break.

We are our own worst enemy,
We are our first line of defense.
If we are not each other's keeper,
How dare we call ourselves sapiens!

Part 17

Sapiens is integration,
Sapiens is assimilation.
Sapiens is declaration of oneness,
Sapiens is defiance of dehydration.

From tribal descendants to global ancestors,
that's the mental shift that defines a human.
There's no greater blasphemy or tragedy,
than a modern human behaving like a caveman.

It's okay if our beliefs differ -
so long as the result is love,
it's okay if the routes differ.

For example, the greatest poet to me,
was, unlike me, a devout believer.

It is through his hateless devotion to god,
Mevlana (Rumi) acted as a poetic beacon of love.
So, I embrace his belief without resistance,
despite having no affinity to supernatural stuff.

Problem is not belief or disbelief,
Real problem is hate born of division.
Divisionists will divide no matter the excuse,
Stand up, not to differences, but to differentiation.

I know a lot of people,
who believe in the supernatural.
Yet I also know for a fact,
that they are good, hateless people.

Illogicality has nothing to do with hate,
Defy acts of hate, not acts of illogicality.
Know the right place to apply your reason,
Often monstrosity comes disguised as rationality.

Rise above rationality,
riding the rays of the heart.
Soar above insensitivity,
rid yourself of all uncharitable dirt.

Raise the world, revive the world,
Shelter the world from all storms.
Envision the world, design the world,
Deliver the world from dusk to dawn.

Seek annihilation for a purpose,
And you'll be resurrected a thousand times.
Live a thousand years without purpose,
You are no more alive than spineless slime.

Purposelessness is lifelessness,
But, purpose of life is chosen by life alone.
Unless you see yourself as a vessel for uplift,
No power can help your powers unfold.

World is but reflection of the individual -
When there is muck inside, outside too there is muck.
Growing big in appearance means nothing,
Heartless giant is nothing but a homunculus.

Hearts on fire bring the world to light,
Backbones on fire strengthen its might.
Reflect and you shall plainly see,
Life set alight is world brought to life.

World lives because you live,
World breathes because you breathe.
When you live and breathe on love alone,
Slowly but surely, peace will be.

Part 18

Peace is not a cause,
Peace is a pause -
Pause in hate and greed,
Pause in gain and loss.

States cannot bring peace,
for state and peace are antithesis of each other.
Move past the state, look into culture -
the world won't have peace
till there is integration amongst cultures.

States rise, states fall,
but cultures are everlasting.
Isms arrive, isms wither,
but human spirit is evergreen.

You don't have to support
the state to love the culture.
You may be deemed enemy of the state,
and still be a hero of the culture.

Heroes of culture are often
branded as enemy of the state.
Because while the state aims for stability,
Heroes of culture humanize the national make.

Culture transcends state,
Liberty transcends law.
Conscience transcends scripture,
Indifference is the main outlaw.

However, one thing you must remember -
There's nothing stagnant about culture,
Culture stagnant is recipe for disaster.
Culture alive is dynamic and evolving,
There is no place for rigidity in culture.

Rigidity is incivility,
Exclusivity is inhumanity.
Reason is civility,
Inclusivity is humanity.

Inclusion is expansion,
Exclusion is contraction.
Expansion is existence,
Contraction is extinction.

Contraction comes in many forms,
not just in the form of ignorance.
Rationality also can cause contraction,
by mechanizing the mind with sheer coldness.

Know the place of rationality,
Use it where it is paramount.
Know also where to put it to rest,
And let the heart lead not logic bound.

Science is not merely about logicality,
Real science is using logic to lift up society.
Just like theology is not merely about memorizing
scripture, real theology is about using the good
from scripture, to elevate all of humanity.

Bad scientist lets science dictate life,
Good scientist uses science to lift up life.
Bad theologian lets scripture dictate life,
Good theologian uses scripture to lift up life.

No matter what field you are in,
Use it as an instrument of uplift.
If life aids not the lift of life,
It is no being but compost heap.

Part 19

There is no handbook to life,
Life is the handbook to everything.
Wield your life as a force for good,
Unfold your vastness in moments fleeting.

Time never runs out, we just run out of
the mind that manufactures time.
Life never runs out, we just run out of
the mind that manufactures all life.

Know mind, you'll know time,
Know mind, you'll know life.
Develop the mind to know the mind,
And you'll know what is human life.

Know life, you'll know love,
Know love, you'll know life.
Know love, my friend, not about love,
know love - and that's the beginning of life.

Sev be insan, sadece sev,
İnsan olarak insanı sev.
Nefreti unut, şöhreti unut,
Her şeyi unutup dünyayı sev.

Ne bahar, ne bulutlar,
her an, her dakika,
yaşamak için sev,
sevmek için yaşa.

When the drive for love overwhelms
the instinct of hate, human being is born.
When the drive for learning overwhelms
the convenience of belief, human being is born.

When the drive for poetic science
grows stronger than ever, human being is born.
When the drive for benevolence fuses
with the science of behavior, human being is born.

When the purpose of hatelessness is
realized by a borderless heart, human being is born.
When economic justice joins hands with
humanitarian science, human being is born.

When a nonsectarian spirit meets with
a world building backbone, human being is born.
When existential questions call for
egalitarian answers, human being is born.

Human is born, not when the water breaks,
Human is born, when the bias breaks.
Person grows, not when the body grows,
But when the mind outgrows fear and prejudices.

Fear and fanaticism are the enemy,
that makes animals out of humans.
States further facilitate fear,
because citizens without fear
are harder to control.

Democracy is but a fancy myth,
All states are secretly dictatorial.
Absolute democracy needs no government,
Existence of government is predicated on control.

That's why nationalist patriotism is such
a big deal - because you cannot justify war,
if your citizens become global humans.
Ergo the state maintains a narrative of fear,
A nation without fear is a nation without borders.

Yet that's precisely what the world needs -
citizens without fear in the course of love.
Write your own narrative with the ink of peace,
and no state, media or cult could divide the world.

Let me rephrase the last bit for perspective.

Write your own narrative with the ink of peace,
and no Sam, Fox or Rome could divide the world.

Part 20

The sun does not have the prehistoric luxury
to distinguish between citizens and aliens.
The sun exists to light up the lives
of anyone and everyone who comes its way.

I must lift up China just as I have lifted America,
I must lift up Russia just as I have lifted Latin America.
Baboons can pick and mix, between this people and that,
Crimson sun of the night sky am I,
I exist to light up the world.

Armor of the world must armor the world,
without bothering with native land and foreign land.
Nationalities are for tribal cavemen,
the entire world is my home, my nation.

Ama a todos, vive para todos,
Vive para amar, ama para vivir.
Amar, vivir, servir, todo mismo,
Vive para servir, sirve para vivir.

I repeat, nationality is for cavemen,
Patriotism is for mindless pest.
What's needed is patriotism for the planet,
Expand yourself beyond sovereignty and state.

Division in any form
is deviation from humanity.
Identity that thrives on division,
must be rejected most enthusiastically.

Defy any government that demands nationalism,
Defy any institution that peddles division.
Place your attention on virtues of universality,
Only then you'll be the pioneer of ascension.

If we cared more about conscience and compassion,
than sovereignty and state, the world would've
had less borders and more bridges.
Nationality is terrorism,
organized religion is organized crime,
if you don't get this, you're the cause
of all geopolitical violence.

To nationalize humanity
is to bring ruin upon humanity.
To doctrinize morality
is to destroy morality.

Morality must come from
the heart, not hagiographies.
Then boil it well in flames of reason,
to rid it of prejudicial impurities.

Prejudice rarely appears as prejudice,
most times they manifest as matters of pride.
Unless the backbone is
strong enough to defy such pride,
you shall be another pawn
in the crowd of tribal termite.

Why are you so afraid to lose
your identity, when none of that
identity is actually yours!
Every identity is mere memory,
when will you grow out of your
reliance on prehistoric shores!

Know your history, for sure,
but how could you let history
dictate the fate of your present!
Keep your history only as history,
not as your whole identity, but
merely a part of your life sapient.

Part 21

Now I am empty,
I don't know what to write.
So I turn off all thought,
And let love lead the ride.

Speak whatever tongue you may,
Breathe whatever breeze you may.
All forces come from nature,
In nature all will fade away.

Saril bana, vurun bana,
Nasıl istiyorsa, hoşgeldin!
Rüyama gel, rüzgarda gel,
Kaderim artık senin kararın.

İnsan çok tanıdık birini değil,
kanına girmiş birini sever.
Hay necesidad de abrazo sin juicio -
Sabes abrazar, no hay necesidad de hablar.

Hug, don't hurt.
Love, don't loathe.
Lift, don't drift.
Grow, don't woe.

Thought takes you only so far,
Heart takes you all the way.
Thought fails where logic fails,
Heart keeps beating, way or no way.

Heart is the potentest power source of all,
Hands are the mightiest tools of all.
Brain is the smartest computer of all,
Backbone is the strongest concrete of all.

With all this power packed within,
Why do you submit to institutional authority!
Bow to wisdom if you have something to learn,
But pledge your allegiance to none but humanity.

In fact, take the term 'authority'
out of your vocabulary altogether.
Absorb excellence and wisdom like
a sponge from wherever you find,
without contributing to yet
another authoritarian disaster.

Be a student and practitioner of excellence,
Practice the craft for the sheer joy of the craft.
Focus less on each other's flaws and shortcomings,
Endeavor to empower each other's good parts.

Shortcoming is not the same as savagery,
Stand up, not to every shortcoming, but to savagery.
In fact, you can never be a first class human being,
till you learn to have some respect for human frailty.

You ask me, is there a perfect soul!
I say, imperfect souls chase perfection,
perfect souls wield their imperfection
as their greatest strength.

When we strengthen another,
we strengthen ourselves.
When we celebrate another,
we celebrate ourselves.

All divide is in the mind,
Mind divided is world divided.
Devoid yourself of such divide,
And you'll have a celebration every day.

Part 22

Ramadan Sonnet

Bismillah-ir-Rahman-ir-Rahim doesn't mean,
God is merciful only to the muslim.
The spirit of godliness that we hold within,
is meant to light up the world as our kin.
Fasting and feasting all turn mere futile choir,
If, for whatever reason, life is distant from life.
Celebration of Ramadan is celebration of rahmat*,
Ramadan without *compassion is Ramadan without life.
Ramadan is not a muslim festival,
Ramadan is a human festival.
Ramadan is a reminder to rekindle our light,
Ramadan is the end of all feelings uncharitable.
None of us will have faith till we wish for
our neighbor as we wish for ourselves (Hadith 13).
The reward for goodness is goodness itself (Q55:60).

When amidst believers,
speak in the tongue of believers.
When amidst atheists,
speak in the tongue of atheists.

But if you find yourself amidst
militants and fundamentalists,
do not speak, just listen,
and you'll learn
how not to be a human being.

Logic doesn't make you
a good person, love does.
Belief doesn't make you
a good person, behavior does.

Love within is the same,
though the expressions may vary.
Look at the entity beyond the expression,
and you'll find yourself in whole of humanity.

Question not, why there is love?
Question instead, why there is hate?
Hate is born of divide,
Erase divide, you erase hate.

Do you have any idea,
how love works?
Me neither.
Think not how love works,
Just give up, and let love work you.

Give up, and let love work you,
Let love reshape your every pore.
Let love mould you like innocent clay,
Let love revive you from your very core.

Let love take away all you are,
so that you may become what you could be.
Resist not the blazing fire of suffering,
the meal gains its proper flavor,
upon being stirred in fire nicely.

Painless love is puppy love,
Adult love is a circle of joyful disasters.
Each disaster paves the way for sunny days,
Each sunrise leads up to the next disaster.

Karanlıksız aşk yalan aşktır,
Karanlıkta bile sevmek, kara sevdadır.
Mutlulukta sevmek herkese kolay,
Felakette sevmek sadece
sarhoş bir aşık için mümkündür.

Amor sin dolor es amor de cachorro.
Sólo un corazón valiente puede
amar a través del cataclismo.

Part 23

To love, you cannot think clear,
To think clear, you mustn't love.
Anybody can love when all is clear,
Only a drunken lover can love
through disaster.

When it's time,
be sober.
When it's love,
go over.

What I say is simple.

Life is short,
Forgive a lot,
Help plenty,
Love like crazy.

Think before you speak,
Reason before you assume.
Learn before you judge,
Wise up, lest your
prejudice is exhumed.

Choose your words carefully,
Moderate your beliefs consciously.
Observe your ignorance cautiously,
Humanize your behavior conscientiously.

I use words to change the world,
Because guns are obsolete.
As a teen I was obsessed with
designing defense tech,
Upon growing up,
I became a vessel for peace.

Peace is possible,
because I am possible.
Peace is possible,
because you are possible.

Never forget,
You are the law,
o brave civilian!
Put your mind to it,
and all is possible.

Discard all shortsightedness,
Do away with all narrowmindedness.
Move high, from "my, my, my",
Be a champion of collective progress!

Vagabond Poet
(Sonnet 1044)

No matter how much
they plagiarize my work,
I won't say a word to condemn.
No matter how much they
monetize solar energy,
you never hear the sun complain!

It's okay that limited minds
got to care about such matter.
What does the ocean care about
a few buckets of stolen water!

I am infinite, I am unbound -
Come, steal all I've got,
strip me of all my legacy!
I started out as a vagabond,
I'll gladly perish in vagabondcy.

140

Part 24

The question is not how much
you have left for yourself!
The question is, how much
more you can give away!

Of course, you gotta provide for your family,
But make sure, that's not all you think about.
You have not one, but two families,
One is your immediate kith and kin,
the other is the world around.

And one who realizes this,
will also realize,
it's not really two,
for we all are but one family.

As a kid I only wanted one thing - immortality!
So I worked at it secretly.

How does a mortal become immortal?
By giving up their mortality
in the cause of humanity.

Wipe out America,
you wipe out Naskar the scientist.
Wipe out Turkey,
you wipe out Naskar the poet.
Wipe out India,
you wipe out Naskar the theologian.
Wipe out Earth,
you wipe out Naskar the humanitarian.

Be a humanitarian,
not a human looking terrier.
Better think and feel before you speak,
than behave as talking derriere.

Some people hate pigs,
Some people love pigs,
Some people behave like pigs.
Some people worship cows,
Some people feast on cows,
Some people just act like cows.

Eat what you like,
Believe what you like.
As long as you don't
behave like pigs and cows,
let no tradition be your guide.

Be your own guide, Be your own light.
You have a head, heart and backbone,
Bring them to use at their fullest might.

Your might is my might,
My might is your might.
When we might up together,
We become a dynamite.

Divided we are incurable,
United we are a miracle.
Segregated we are suited apes,
Integrated we are sapiens noble.

Blood is no measure of nobility,
Behavior alone makes a person noble.
Those who still obsess with pedigree,
are the last people to heed on what's noble.

One of the greatest tragedies
of society is the blood delusion.
Those who still suffer from it are
prehistoric remnants of uncivilization.

Let them be as they are, but
pay not much heed to what they say.
Tribal beliefs make tribal society,
accept such tribals as children,
and keep walking your human way.

Part 25

148

There is no such thing as human tribe,
Just like there is no animal society.
You either belong to the animal tribe,
Or you are member of the human society.

The right phrases are,
human society and animal tribe,
animal species and humankind.
Only a human from humankind,
can develop this simple sight.

Instinct is animal,
Insight is human.
Self-preservation is animal,
World-preservation is human.

Division is animal,
Integration is human.
Integrate or disintegrate,
It's all your decision.

Ask not, is there life after death!
Ask instead, is there life in existence divided!

Be the hope to the world unfree,
Be the heart to the world unheard.
Don't be a dilettante in a militant world,
Make a tent out of your life, and shelter those
devastated by fanatic nutters.

Shield the world from fanatics,
Restrain the fanatics without harming them.
Put an end to the cycle of violence and vengeance,
Write a new paradigm of nonviolent bravery,
without showing any sign of compliant indifference.

Fanatics thrive on indifference of the commoner.
Till the commoners declare peace against fanaticism,
hate will continue one way or another.

By thought, by heart, by word, by act,
let the fanatics know
that the days of division are long gone.
Silence on your part is exactly what
has kept them in business for so long.

Accept no excuse for inhumanity, be it
scripture based, logic based, or ideology based.
Accept no division no matter the form,
cut off all ties that keep you internally dead.

You can be ignorant, and still be alive,
But there is no life where there is division.
Ignorance is treated easily with curiosity,
But there is no cure for empty intellectualization.

When prejudice comes disguised as intellect,
Such intellect only leads to paralysis mental.
Prejudice is paralysis,
and paralysis cures no paralysis,
unless you realize you're a walking cripple.

There is no cripple in body,
there is only cripple in mind.
Even without arms and legs,
mind can still travel far,
but when the mind is crippled,
none can stop time falling behind.

Cripple aware is cripple cured,
Prejudice aware is prejudice restrained.
Ignorance aware is ignorance contained,
Blindness aware is blindness overwhelmed.

Part 26

With all our eyes, we don't see.
With all our ears, we don't hear.
With all our tongues, we don't speak.
With all our limbs, we still disappear.

We turn our eyes where we need to see,
We shut our ears where we need to listen.
We chain our tongue where we need a voice,
We freeze our feet where we need movement.

It's time to thaw the freeze,
It's time to break the silence.
It's time we hearken to cries,
It's time we walk as guardians.

Guardians get scared too,
Guardians have prejudice too.
But unlike the savages of modern times,
Guardians constantly reshape their mind anew.

Be less biased than you were yesterday,
Be less prejudiced than you were yesterday.
Be not hesitant to discard the junk,
Even if at some point they'd seen venerated days.

Humankind is the supreme truth,
All other truths are expendable.
Nourish any truth that
facilitates human welfare,
Destroy all truths that make mind
paranoid and mental.

We learnt so much!

We learnt how to fly like birds,
We learnt how to swim like fish,
Yet we haven't learnt to love like human.

What's the point in all
these intellectual endeavors,
if they couldn't teach us
how to treat people with dignity!
We have found extensions
for every faculty, yet
the heart remains anemic of amity.

Stop focusing on extending your personality,
Place your attention on extending your humanity.
What's the point in achieving longevity,
if human life reeks of rotten inhumanity!

Long life or short life,
It's all useless without love.
Better love and die in five days,
than live coldly for a thousand years.

Measure of life is not years,
Measure of life is love.
Love is the only measure,
which empowers us to take
the rightful measures.

What is right, what is wrong,
Intellect will never show the way.
Intellect dwells in the domain of facts,
Right and wrong transcend all factual ways.

Rightness comes from wholeness,
Where there is no wholeness,
there is no rightness.
Intellect, like ignorance,
often leads us astray
from the path of humanness.

Be a human being first,
then a person of intellect if you may.
Observe all with your life rooted in love,
only then your brain will show the right way.

Heart's way is the right way,
All else is either aid or impediment.
If it aids your heart embrace it fully,
But dump it fast if it causes impediment.

Heart is not to be a dumpyard of division,
Heart is the miracle ground of assimilation.
Hate is an insult on the existence of heart,
Be heartful first, and there'll be mindful ascension.

Let the heart be full with heart,
Heart united is mind ignited.
Mindfulness is simply a byproduct
of the sacred act of heartfulness.

Where heart begins, there life begins,
Heartlessness is lifelessness.
Set out in the course of heart,
And life will come chasing,
quite like a happy accident.

Ask not, where you begin!
Ask instead, where you belong!
Belonging is the beginning,
Where you belong, there you're born.

BIBLIOGRAPHY

Archer M., (2000), Being Human: The Problem of Agency. Cambridge University Press.

Adolphs R (2003) Cognitive neuroscience of human social behaviour. Nature Rev Neurosci 4: 165–178.

Adolphs R, Tranel D, Damasio AR (2003) Dissociable neural systems for recognizing emotions. Brain Cogn 52: 61–69.

Andresen, Jensine, and Robert Forman, eds. Cognitive Models and Spiritual Maps. Bowling Green, Ohio: Imprint Academic, 2000.

Bernstein R.J., (1971), Praxis and Action: Contemporary Philosophies of Human Activity. Philadelphia: University of Pennsylvania Press.

Bernstein R.J., (1976), The Restructuring Social and Political Thought.

Bogen, J.E.(1995a), 'On the neurophysiology of consciousness: Part I. An overview', Consciousness and Cognition, 4.

Bogen, J.E. (1995b), 'On the neurophysiology of consciousness: Part II. Constraining the semantic problem', Consciousness and Cognition, 4.

Bremner, J. D., R. Soufer, et al. (2001). "Gender differences in cognitive and neural correlates of remembrance of emotional words." Psychopharmacol Bull 35 (3).

Brothers, L. (2002). The social brain: A project for integrating primate behavior and neurophysiology in a new domain. In J. T. Cacioppo et al. (Eds.), Foundations in neuroscience. Cambridge, MA: MIT Press.

Buss, D. D. (2003). Evolutionary Psychology: The New Science of Mind, 2nd ed. New York: Allyn & Bacon.

Buss, D. M. (1989). "Conflict between the sexes: Strategic interference and the evocation of anger and upset." J Pers Soc Psychol 56 (5).

Buss, D. M. (1995). "Psychological sex differences. Origins through sexual selection." Am Psychol 50 (3).

Buss, D. M., and D. P. Schmitt (1993). "Sexual strategies theory: An evolutionary perspective on human mating." Psychol Rev 100 (2).

Chomsky Noam, (2016) Who Rules the World?

Churchland, P.S. (1986), Neurophilosophy (Cambridge, MA: The MIT Press).

Churchland, P.S. & Ramachandran, V.S. (1993), 'Filling in: Why Dennett is wrong', in Dennett and His Critics:

Demystifying Mind, ed. B. Dahlbom (Oxford: Blackwell Scientific Press).

Churchland, P.S., Ramachandran, V.S. & Sejnowski, T.J. (1994), 'A critique of pure vision', in Large- scale Neuronal Theories of the Brain, ed. C. Koch & J.L. Davis (Cambridge, MA: The MIT Press).

Crick, F. (1994), The Astonishing Hypothesis: The Scientific Search for the Soul (New York: Simon and Schuster).

Crick, F. (1996), 'Visual perception: rivalry and consciousness', Nature, 379.

Crick, F. & Koch, C. (1992), 'The problem of consciousness', Scientific American, 267.

d'Aquili, Eugene. "Senses of Reality in Science and Religion." Zygon 17, no 4 (1982) d'Aquili, Eugene. "The Biopsychological Determinants of Religious Ritual Behavior." Zygon 10, no. 1 (1975)

d'Aquili, Eugene. "The Myth-Ritual Complex: A Biogenetic Structural Analysis." Zygon 18, no. 3 (1983)

d'Aquili, Eugene, and Andrew Newberg. The Mystical Mind: Probing the Biology of Religious Experience. Minneapolis: Fortress Press, 1999.

Damasio, A. (1994) Descartes' Error: Emotion, Reason and the Human Brain. New York, Putnams.

Damasio, A. (1999) The Feeling of What Happens: Body, Emotion and the Making of Consciousness. London, Heinemann.

Darwin, C. (1859) On the Origin of Species by Means of Natural Selection. London, Murray.

Darwin, C. (1871) The Descent of Man and Selection in Relation to Sex. London, John Murray.

Dawkins, R. (1976) The Selfish Gene. Oxford, Oxford University Press; a new edition, with additional material, was published in 1989.

Dewhurst, Kenneth, and A. W. Beard. "Sudden Religious Conversions in Temporal Lobe Epilepsy." British Journal of Psychiatry 117 (1970)

Dewhurst K, Beard AW. Sudden religious conversions in temporal lobe epilepsy. 1970 Epilepsy Behav 2003

Devinsky O, Lai G. Spirituality and religion in epilepsy. Epilepsy Behav 2008.

E. Horvitz, "One Hundred Year Study on Artificial Intelligence: Reflections and Framing," ed: Stanford University, 2014.

Eckhart Meister, Selected Writings

Farah, M.J. (1989), 'The neural basis of mental imagery', Trends in Neurosciences, 10.

Freud, S. "Selected papers on hysteria and other psychoneuroses" Journal of Nervous and Mental Disease 1909.

Freud, S. "The Origin and Development of Psychoanalysis", 1910

Freud, S. "Psychopathology of everyday life", 1914

Freud, S. "Beyond the Pleasure Principle", 1920

Frith, C.D. & Dolan, R.J. (1997), 'Abnormal beliefs: Delusions and memory', Paper presented at the May, 1997, Harvard Conference on Memory and Belief.

Gay, Volney, ed. Neuroscience and Religion. Plymouth, UK: Lexington Books, 2009.

Gazzaniga, M. S. (1985). The social brain. New York: Basic Books.

Gazzaniga, M.S. (1993), 'Brain mechanisms and conscious experience', Ciba Foundation Symposium, 174.

Geschwind N. "Behavioural changes in temporal lobe epilepsy". Psychol Med. 1979.

Gellhorn, E., Kiely, W.F. "Mystical states of consciousness: neurophysiological and clinical aspects." J Nerv Ment Dis. 1972;154:399-405.

Gilbert SL, Dobyns WB, Lahn BT (2005) Genetic links between brain development and brain evolution. Nat Rev Genet 6.

Gray JA. The Psychology of Fear and Stress. 2nd ed. New York, NY: Cambridge University Press; 1988.

Gloor, P. (1992), 'Amygdala and temporal lobe epilepsy', in The Amygdala: Neurobiological Aspects of Emotion, Memory and Mental

Dysfunction, ed J.P. Aggleton (New York: Wiley-Liss).

Gross CG, Rocha-Miranda CE, Bender DB (1972) Visual properties of neurons in the inferotemporal cortex of the macaque. J Neurophysiol 35: 96–111.

Guevara Che, The Motorcycle Diaries, 1992

Hardy, G. H. (1940). Ramanujan. Cambridge: Cambridge University Press.

Hall, Daniel, Keith Meador, and Harold Koenig. "Measuring Religiousness in Health Research: Review and Critique." Journal of Religion and Health 47, no. 2 (2008)

Harris, Sam, Jonas Kaplan, Ashley Curiel, Susan Bookheimer, Marco Iacoboni, and Mark Cohen. "The Neural Correlates of Religious and Nonreligious Belief." PLoS One 4, no. 10 (October 1, 2009)

Halgren, E. (1992), 'Emotional neurophysiology of the amygdala within the context of human cognition', in The Amygdala: Neurobiological Aspects of Emotion, Memory and Mental Dysfunction, ed J.P. Aggleton (New York: Wiley-Liss).

Halligan PW, Fink GR, Marshal JC, Vallar G. 2003. Spatial cognition: evidence from visual neglect. Trends Cogn Sci.

Handbook of Emotions, Edited by Michael Lewis, Jeannette M. Haviland-Jones, and Lisa Feldman Barrett, The Guilford Press; 3rd edition (2010).

Hameroff, S.R. and Penrose, R. (1996) Conscious events as orchestrated space-time selections. Journal of Consciousness Studies 3(1), 36-53; also reprinted in J. Shear (ed.) (1997) Explaining Consciousness-The Hard Problem. Cambridge, MA, MIT Press, 177-95.

Harding, D.E. (1961) On Having no Head: Zen and the Re-Discovery of the Obvious. London, Buddhist Society.

Hardy, A. (1979) The Spiritual Nature of Man: A Study of Contemporary Religious Experience. Oxford, Clarendon Press.

Harre, R. and Gillett, G. (1994) The Discursive Mind. Thousand Oaks, CA, Sage.

Haugeland, J. (ed.) (1997) Mind Design II: Philosophy, Psychology, Artificial Intelligence. Cambridge, MA, MIT Press.

Hauser, M.D. (2000) Wild Minds: What Animals Really Think. New York, Henry Holt and Co.; London, Penguin.

Hilgard, E.R. (1986) Divided Consciousness: Multiple Controls in Human Thought and Action. New York, Wiley.

Hilton, E.N., Lundberg, T.R. Transgender Women in the Female Category of Sport: Perspectives on Testosterone Suppression and Performance Advantage. Sports Med 51, 199–214 (2021).

Hitler, Adolf. Mein Kampf, 1925

Hodgson, R. (1891) A case of double consciousness. Proceedings of the Society for Psychical Research 7, 221-58.

Hofstadter, D.R. and Dennett, D.C. (eds) (1981) The Mind's I: Fantasies and Reflections on Self and Soul. London, Penguin.

Holland, J. (ed.) (2001) Ecstasy: The Complete Guide: A Comprehensive Look at the Risks and Benefits of MDMA. Rochester, VT, Park Street Press.

Holmes, D.S. (1987) The influence of meditation versus rest on physiological arousal. In M. West (ed.)

The Psychology of Meditation. Oxford, Clarendon Press, 81-103.

Holmstrom, David. 1992, Christian Science Monitor

Holloway RL (1996) Evolution of the human brain. In: Lock A, Peters CR (eds) Handbook of human symbolic evolution. Oxford University Press, Oxford

Jeannerod M (1988) The neural and behavioural organization of goal-directed movements. Clarendon Press, Oxford.

Johnson-Frey SH, Maloof FR, Newman-Norlund R, Farrer C, Inati S, Grafton ST (2003) Actions or hand-objects interactions? Human inferior frontal cortex and action observation. Neuron 39: 1053–1058.

Jackson, F. (1982) Epiphenomenal qualia. Philosophical Quarterly 32, 127-36.

James, W. (1890) The Principles of Psychology (2 volumes). London, Macmillan.

James, W. (1902) The Varieties of Religious Experience: A Study in Human Nature. New York and London, Longmans, Green and Co.

Jansen, K. (2001) Ketamine: Dreams and Realities. Sarasota, FL, Multidisciplinary Association for Psychedelic Studies.

Jay, M. (ed.) (1999) Artificial Paradises: A Drugs Reader. London, Penguin.

Jaynes, J. (1976) The Origin of Consciousness in the Breakdown of the Bicameral Mind. New York, Houghton Mifflin.

Kandel, E. R. In Search of Memory: The Emergence of a New Science of Mind, W. W. Norton & Company (2007).

Kandel E. R. Schwartz JH, Jessel TM. Principles of neural sciences. New York; McGraw Hill, 2000.

Kanwisher, N. (2001) Neural events and perceptual awareness. Cognition 79, 89-113; also reprinted inS. Dehaene (ed.) The Cognitive Neuroscience of Consciousness. Cambridge, MA, MIT Press, 89-113.

Kihlstrom, J.F. (1996) Perception without awareness of what is perceived, learning without awareness of what is learned. In M. Velmans (ed.) The Science of Consciousness. London, Routledge, 23-46.

Kosslyn, S.M. (1980) Image and Mind. Cambridge, MA, Harvard University Press.

Kosslyn, S.M. (1988) Aspects of a cognitive neuroscience of mental imagery. Science 240, 1621-6.

Kjaer, Troels, Camilla Bertelsen, Paola Piccini, David Brooks, Jorgen Alving, and Hans Lou. "Increased Dopamine Tone during Meditation- Induced Change of Consciousness." Cognitive Brain Research 13, no. 2 (April 2002)

Kölmel HW. 1985. Complex visual hallucinations in the hemianopic field. J Neurol Neurosurg Psychiatry.

Koenig, Harold. "Research on Religion, Spirituality, and Mental Health: A Review." Canadian Journal of Psychiatry 54, no. 5 (May 2009)

Koenig, Harold, ed. Handbook of Religion and Mental Health. San Diego, CA: Academic Press, 1998

Kraepelin E. Psychiatry: A Textbook for Students and Physicians. New York, NY: Science History Publications; 1990.

Lauglin, Charles, John McManus, and Eugene d'Aquili. Brain, Symbol, and Experience. 2nd ed. New York: Columbia University Press, 1992

Lakoff, G. and M. Johnson (1999). Philosophy in the flesh. Basic Books: New York.

LeDoux, J. E. (1996). The emotional brain. New York: Simon & Schuster.

LeDoux, J.E. (1992), 'Emotion and the amygdala', in The Amygdala: Neurobiological Aspects of Emo- tion, Memory and Mental Dysfunction, ed J.P. Aggleton (New York: Wiley-Liss).

Levin, D.T. and Simons, D.J. (1997) Failure to detect changes to attended objects in motion pictures. Psychonomic Bulletin and Review 4, 501-6.

Levine,J. (1983) Materialism and qualia: the explanatory gap. Pacific Philosophical Quarterly 64, 354-61.

Levine,J. (2001) Purple Haze: The Puzzle of Consciousness. New York, Oxford University Press. Levine, S. (1979) A Gradual Awakening. New York, Doubleday.

Levinson, B.W. (1965) States of awareness during general anaesthesia. British Journal of Anaesthesia 37, 544-6.

Lewicki, P., Czyzewska, M. and Hoffman, H. (1987) Unconscious acquisition of complex procedural knowledge. Journal of Experimental Psychology: Learning, Memory and Cognition 13, 523-30.

Naskar, Abhijit. "What is Mind?", 2016

Naskar, Abhijit. "Love, God & Neurons: Memoir of A Scientist who found himself by getting lost", 2016

Naskar, Abhijit. "Principia Humanitas", 2017

Naskar, Abhijit. "We Are All Black: A Treatise on Racism", 2017

Naskar, Abhijit. "Either Civilized or Phobic: A Treatise on Homosexuality", 2017

Naskar, Abhijit. "Build Bridges not Walls: In the name of Americana", 2018

Naskar, Abhijit. "Citizens of Peace: Beyond the Savagery of Sovereignty", 2019

Naskar, Abhijit. "The Constitution of The United Peoples of Earth", 2019

Naskar, Abhijit. "Mission Reality", 2019

Naskar, Abhijit. "Good Scientist: When Science and Service Combine", 2020

Newberg, Andrew, and Jeremy Iversen. "The Neural Basis of the Complex Mental Task of Meditation: Neurotransmitter and Neurochemical Considerations." Medical Hypotheses 61, no. 2 (2003).

Newberg, Andrew. "How God Changes Your Brain: An Introduction to Jewish Neurotheology", CCAR

Journal: The Reform Jewish Quarterly, Winter 2016.

Newberg, Andrew, and Stephanie Newberg. "A Neuropsychological Perspective on Spiritual Development." In Handbook of Spiritual Development in Childhood and Adolescence, edited by Eugene Roehlkepartain, Pamela King, Linda Wagener, and Peter Benson. London: Sage Publications, Inc., 2005

Newberg, Andrew. "The Neurotheology Link An Intersection Between Spirituality and Health", Alternative and Complimentary Therapies, Vol 21 No 1, February 2015.

Newberg, Andrew, Nancy Wintering, Dharma Khalsa, Hannah Roggenkamp, and Mark Waldman. "Meditation Effects on Cognitive Function and Cerebral Blood Flow in Subjects with Memory Loss: A Preliminary Study." Journal of Alzheimer's Disease 20, no. 2 (2010)

Nash, M. (1995), 'Glimpses of the mind', Time.

Nesse RM. Proximate and evolutionary studies of anxiety, stress and depression: synergy at the interface. Neurosci Biobehav Rev. 1999;23:895-903.

Nicolelis, Miguel. (2011) "Beyond Boundaries: The New Neuroscience of Connecting Brains with Machines--- and How It Will Change Our Lives", Times Books

O'Hara, K. and Scutt, T. (1996) There is no hard problem of consciousness. Journal of Consciousness Studies 3(4), 290-302, reprinted in J. Shear (ed.) (1997) Explaining Consciousness. Cambridge, MA, MIT Press, 69-82.

O'Regan, J.K. and Noe, A. (2001) A sensorimotor account of vision and visual consciousness. Behavioral and Brain Sciences 24(5), 883-917.

Ornstein, R.E. (1977) The Psychology of Consciousness (2nd edn). New York, Harcourt.

Ornstein, R.E. (1986) The Psychology of Consciousness (3rd edn). New York, Pehguin.

Ornstein, R.E. (1992) The Evolution of Consciousness. New York, Touchstone.

Penfield W, Faulk ME (1955) The insula: further observations on its function. Brain 78: 445– 470.

Penrose, R. (1994), Shadows of the Mind (Oxford: Oxford University Press).

Penrose, R. (1989), The Emperor's New Mind: Concerning Computers, Minds and The Laws of Physics (Oxford: Oxford University Press).

Persinger, "'I would kill in God's name' role of sex, weekly church attendance, report of a religious experience and limbic lability" Perceptual and Motor Skills 1997.

Persinger "Experimental simulation of the God experience" Neurotheology 2003.

Persinger, Corradini, Clement, Keaney, et al "Neurotheology and its convergence with neuroquantology" NeuroQuantology 2010.

Persinger. "The neuropsychiatry of paranormal experiences". J Neuropsychiatry Clin Neurosci 2001.

Persinger. "Neuropsychological bases of god beliefs", New York: Praeger, 1987

Persinger. "Temporal lobe epileptic signs and correlative behaviors displayed by normal populations", Journal of General Psychology, 1986

Perry BD, Pollard R. Homeostasis, stress, trauma, and adaptation. A neurodevelopmental view of childhood trauma. Child Adolesc Psychiatr Clin N Am. 1998;7:33.

Ramachandran VS. Behavioral and magnetoencephalographic correlates of plasticity in the adult human brain. Proc Natl Acad Sci USA 1993; 90: 10413–20.

Ramachandran VS. Plasticity and functional recovery in neurology. Clin Med 2005; 5: 368–73.

Rock I, Victor J. Vision and touch: an experimentally created conflict between the two senses. Science 1964; 143: 594–6.

Roberts, TA; Smalley, J; Ahrendt, D (December 2020). "Effect of gender affirming hormones on athletic performance in transwomen and transmen: implications for sporting organisations and legislators". British Journal of Sports Medicine. 55 (11): 577–583

Royet JP, Plailly J, Delon-Martin C, Kareken DA, Segebarth C (2003) fMRI of emotional responses to odors: influence of hedonic valence and judgment, handedness, and gender. Neuroimage 20: 713–728.

Rozin R Haidt J and McCauley CR (2000) Disgust. In: Lewis M, Haviland-Jones JM (eds) Handbook of Emotion. 2nd Edition. Guilford Press, New York, pp 637–653.

Saxe R, Carey S, Kanwisher N (2004) Understanding other minds: linking developmental psychology and functional neuroimaging. Annu Rev Psychol 55: 87–124.

S. J. Russell and P. Norvig, Artificial intelligence: a modern approach (3rd edition): Prentice Hall, 2009.

Singer T, Seymour B, O'Doherty J, Kaube H, Dolan RJ, Frith CD (2004) Empathy for pain involves the affective but not the sensory components of pain. Science 303: 1157–1162.

Smith A (1759) The theory of moral sentiments (ed. 1976). Clarendon Press, Oxford.

Schilling, Vincent. 2017, indian country today

Stein, Stephen K. 2017, The Sea in World History: Exploration, Travel, and Trade

Tesla N. "My Inventions", 1919

T. R. Society, "Machine learning: the power and promise of computers that learn by example," ed. The Royal Society, 2017.

Tomasello M, Call J (1997) Primate cognition. Oxford University Press, Oxford

www.ingramcontent.com/pod-product-compliance
Lightning Source LLC
Chambersburg PA
CBHW051049250726
48656CB00001B/218